Copyright

Introduction To Search Engine Optimization

Creating and publishing a website is no longer a mysterious, cryptic task that is reserved only for computer geeks. Nowadays, virtually everyone and their dog has their own website. Anyone wanting a piece of the virtual pie can easily sign up for a free Blogger blog in about five minutes. In addition, there are lots of WYSIWYG editors available that make creating a beautiful, interactive website a very simple drag & drop process.

So that's the easy part. The difficulty lies in getting your website seen! With the internet's estimated 20 billion webpages, how on earth can you attempt to rise above obscurity and become well-known and famous in your niche?

The answer lies in search engine optimization. SEO can be defined as the process of driving traffic to your website organically (unpaid) from the search engines. In order to get the search engine bots to notice your site and include it in the results pages, you'll need to work on these three components:

1. Making sure your content is relevant to the keyword phrases being searched

2. Optimizing your website with keywords and linking structures

3. Building powerful inbound links to your website from others in your niche

If you want massive exposure for your website, you need it to rank on the first page of Google for several different keyword phrases. 90% of internet users do not browse beyond the first page of results, so don't settle for being on the second or third page and only getting a tiny sliver of the traffic that you could be getting.

Unfortunately, no one makes it to the #1 spot on Google overnight (unless there happens to be no competition whatsoever –which is highly unlikely for any keyword phrase that gets a decent amount of searches). Unlike "instant" methods like PPC (pay per click), search engine optimization takes a lot of time and effort. Think of PPC as the hustle and bustle of the big city. SEO on the other hand, is like a rural Southern town where progress moves slow and steady like molasses.

Marketers who choose to focus on SEO rather than driving traffic through PPC or other means acknowledge the fact that it takes time. If you are impatient or give up easily, perhaps SEO may not be the right method for you to drive traffic to your website. No worries!

But for those of you that want to learn about SEO, read on. The fundamentals are really quite simple. The first step is learning. The second step is implementing. If you can do those two things, you've got it made!

How Search Engines Work

You see it and use it multiple times throughout the day, but do you know how it works?

Surprisingly, many webmasters severely lack knowledge about one of the most important aspects of the internet –the search engines! We all know they exist, we know people use them, and we know that they drive traffic to our websites. But few people actually carry an understanding about how they work.
If you can educate yourself about the way search engines function, you'll be more capable of optimizing your site properly.

Search engines send automated "bots" to "crawl" the web through hyperlinks.

As we'll discuss later, without external hyperlinks to your website, the bots really have no way of finding your website. It's still possible that they'll discover your site eventually, but without some kind of effort on your part, it may be unlikely.

Only about half of the existing pages on the internet have been crawled by the search engines, if that gives you any indication of the importance of backlinks.

Once the bots crawl your website, it becomes indexed in a huge database along with all the other indexed pages on the internet. There are literally billions of pages stored in this database. Yet, as you've probably noticed, it takes barely a second or two to get results after performing a search.

When searches are made, the engine quickly scans through relevant documents and provides results based on the most accurate possible matches. Generally a match is determined by the presence of that particular keyword on the webpage. Thus, on-page optimization is extremely important.

Google and the other search engines will provide differing results depending on whether you type the phrase as-is (purple umbrellas), in quotes ("purple umbrellas"), with the + symbol (purple + umbrellas), or other variations.

After the SE has found matches for the search query, a special algorithm scans each of the results to determine relevance to the keyword phrase. Results are provided to the user in order from most relevant to least relevant.

So what can you learn from this information? A few things:

1. Your page must be relevant to the search term (listing the keyword several times throughout the course of the website, on-site optimization)

2. You need external hyperlinks (backlinks) pointing to your website to act as a "gateway" for the bots to access your site.

As far as relevance goes, Google and the other search engines take all of these into consideration:

1. On-site optimization

1. Age of the domain (the older the better)

2. Page Rank (PR)

3. Alexa ranking (the 'popularity' of your website based on the amount of traffic it gets)

4. Number of backlinks, particularly from high PR authority websites that are related to your website (if you have a blog about real estate, a high PR link from a real estate website will be more valuable than a high PR link from a website about dog grooming)

5. Linking structure of the website (easy navigation)

So looking at all of these factors, you can see why Amazon.com would take the #1 spot for "buy books" rather than your three-week-old Blogger blog with 4 backlinks.

Stumbling Blocks for the Search Engines

Sometimes the search engines are prevented from crawling your website for one reason or another. You'll want to make sure you eliminate these.

1. Your site requires a cookie for navigation. Bots can't carry cookies the way a regular browser user can.

2. Framed websites. Back in the day (10+ years ago) when I first started designing & programming websites, I loved using frames. But I had no idea that it would hinder my sites' ability to be ranked in the search engines.

3. Long, complicated URLs such as http://www.website.com/page.php?ID=HuUj=987sj=%site%

4. Login pages

5. Redirect pages (Google hates these)

6. Poor linking structure on your website. Each page on your domain should be linked to from the home page (or a sitemap) or the bots may have a difficult time crawling it (because they won't be able to find it). Ideally, you would like to have a very convenient linking structure, in which each page on your domain is accessible from every other page. This is why Wordpress blogs are favored by the

1. search engines, because their layout allows for this kind of linking structure.

2. You accidentally have the "I would like to block search engines" option selected in the "Privacy" tab in your Wordpress dashboard. Sometimes this option is selected automatically, so always double-check that it is turned off. Similar options exist for other sites like Blogger.

3. You have a robots.txt file preventing the search engines from crawling certain pages. Usually this is done purposefully to prevent unwanted content from being indexed, but sometimes it might be a mistake.

4. Your page is heavily coded with Javascript or contains Flash as its primary method of delivering content.

Keyword Research

If you want your website to rank in the search engines, you'll need to optimize it for particular keyword phrases. Keyword research is the process of finding out which keywords will be the easiest and most beneficial to optimize for.

Generally, you'll be looking at two things:

1. Search volume: How many people search for the keyword in a given month.

2. Competition: How many competing websites are also optimized for this keyword phrase.

Why is keyword research important? Well, you can't just pick some keywords and keyword phrases off the top of your head and expect to easily rank for them. If your website is just getting off the ground, you will find it exceptionally difficult to rank for a keyword like "lose weight" or "quit smoking" or even "cat litter".

However, if you conduct proper keyword research, you may be able to find similar keyword phrases that have a decent search volume and little competition. Those are the keywords that you want to target.

I could probably go on and on for one hundred pages about keyword research, but I know you have a busy schedule, so I'm just going to get straight to the point.

To easily conduct keyword research (for free), all you need are two resources at your disposal: The Google Adwords Keyword Tool, and the Google search engine itself.

Open up the Keyword Tool and input your desired keywords. How do you know which keywords to list? Well, let's say you have a website about jewelry. The keyword phrases you choose could be:

buy homemade jewelry
buy homemade necklaces
buy homemade earrings
online jewelry store

Basically, anything related to the content of your website. Generally, the more targeted your keywords are, the better. So if you specialize in turquoise jewelry only, don't bother optimizing for "jewelry" (an exceptionally hard keyword to rank for) –just "turquoise jewelry".

Additionally, don't try to rank for "pearl jewelry" if that's not what your website covers. You want to attract visitors who are specifically looking for "turquoise jewelry" – they will come to your website and see that you are offering them exactly what they are looking for. The overall quality of your traffic will be better and your conversions will be higher.

Click "Get keyword ideas" and you'll be given a long list of related keyword phrases and their search numbers.

Browse through the keyword list and copy down all the keyword phrases that interest you. Generally it's safe to assume that the higher the search volume, the higher the competition, and vice versa. However, this isn't always the case. It's still possible to stumble upon some real gems –keywords with high search volume and little competition.

Let's take a look at this keyword: discount jewelry store. As you can see, it gets 1600 searches per month.

Now go to Google and type it in with quotes, like this: "discount jewelry store"

The quotes tell Google to only show websites that are optimized for the entire keyword phrase, in order. Without quotes, Google searches for all websites that contain the words discount, jewelry, and store, but not necessarily together, and not necessarily in order. So keeping the phrase in quotes is important because it'll give you a more accurate idea of the competition.

As you can see, Google tells us that there are 19,600 competing websites for this keyword phrase. Generally anything under 50,000 is considered pretty good. The lower the better.

Another search you can do is allintitle: "discount jewelry store" and allinanchor: "discount jewelry store".

The first tells you how many websites are optimized with the keyword phrase in the title and the second tells you how many contain the keyword as anchor text in a link. This, in a sense, is your "true" competition, because these people purposely optimizing for your keyword.

Finally, it's important to look at the specific pages that turn up in the top 10 –20 results. Check their Page Rank. You can download a free plugin for Firefox called "Seo For Firefox". There will be a tiny icon at the bottom of your browser that will tell you the PR of any website you're browsing.

It's also important to see what KIND of pages show up in the results. Are they high authority domain names like Amazon, Ebay, etc? Secondary pages (http://www.website.com/discount-jewelry-store.html)?

The best way to tell if a keyword will be easy to rank for is to look for Web 2.0 sites, social bookmarks, and RSS feeds in the top 10. Ezinearticles, GoArticles, Weebly, Squidoo, Hubpages, Livejournal, Wordpress, Blogger, and Quizilla are all examples of Web 2.0 sites.

Furthermore, keep an eye out for results like this:

This is a page from a social bookmarking website. Other sites like this include Mixx, Digg, Propeller, Reddit, and delicious. Also look for Yahoo! Answers and Youtube videos.

If your search (without quotes) looks something like the screenshot below, you've probably found a winner. It doesn't necessarily mean that you won't have to work hard or face challenges, but it's certainly a lot easier to beat these types of websites than it is to beat high authority aged domain names with lots of backlinks.

So there you have it: a very very BASIC guide to keyword research and competition analysis. Once you've found a suitable keyword or keywords, you'll be ready to perform some on-site optimization.

On-Site Optimization

The process of on-site optimization is quite simple. By following these easy steps, you'll be vastly improving your website's search engine friendliness.

Just remember: on-site optimization is important, but don't go overboard. You still want your website to be attractive and comprehensible to actual human visitors. If you go crazy with optimization, try to unnaturally place keywords in sentences where they don't belong, and generally compromise the quality of your site just to look good to the search engines, you'll be making a huge mistake.

It doesn't matter if you rank on page 1 and get 800 visitors a day. If your visitors can't read your website and don't enjoy the experience, all of that traffic will ultimately mean nothing.

But I digress...

You want your keyword(s) to appear:

In the Title

A good title might be: "Discount Jewelry Store –Discount Turquoise Jewelry, Discount Gold

Jewelry". You have your "main" keyword phrase first, followed by a couple secondary keyword phrases. If this page shows up in the results, the keyword that the person searched for will be in bold. Additionally, if you are trying to rank a "deep page" (as in, not the main page) include your main keyword in that title as well ("Best Discount Jewelry Prices – Discount Jewelry Store").

Make sure the titles for each of your pages are unique and relevant to the content being displayed. Avoid extremely long titles, as Google will cut them off. Avoid "keyword stuffing" as well –jamming as many keywords as possible into the title. Google may categorize your site as spam.

In the Body

The keywords need to appear in the body of your website several times. This is often referred to as "keyword density". A good keyword density to aim for is 2-3%. Less than that may not be enough, more than that may be treading on spammy ground.

One great free tool you can use is DupeFreePro. Simply copy and paste all the text on your website into this program and it'll tell you exactly what your keyword density is.

You can also use it to check for duplicate content, hence the name.

Include your keyword at least 3-4 times throughout the actual content –once in the first sentence if possible, a couple times throughout the paragraphs, and once in the last sentence. Emphasizing the keyword through bolding or italicizing may be a good idea. Include your keyword in the H1 tags as well, and at least once in the anchor text of a link.

In the "Title" attribute of Images

If you have images on your website, adding your keyword to the Title attribute may help your images rank in the Google Image search.

<img src="jewelry.jpg" title="Discount Jewelry Store">

In the Domain Name

I would highly recommend including your primary keyword in your domain name, if you haven't already purchased one. Google places a lot of importance on domain names with keywords in them, especially if it's like this: http://www.keyword.com.

Of course, it may not be possible to purchase a .com domain with the keyword of your choice.

Check for the .net and .org alternatives, or you could put a dash in between the words of your keyword phrase. Limit it to only one or two dashes, however. Any more than that and your domain name could look spammy.

Another option is adding a prefix or a suffix. Generally suffixes are preferred because you want your keyword to be first. So instead of www.keyword.com, you could make it www.keywordblog.com, www.keywordsite.com, www.keywordstore.com, etc.

As far as prefixes go, many webmasters like to add "my" or "the" to their domain name, like www.mydiscountjewelrystore.com.

Meta Tags

Meta tags have been around since the old days of the internet. Back then they carried a lot of weight, but in recent years have become less important. The search engines realized that meta tags were being abused by spammers, and now Google does not really place any importance on the tags except for the description.

Using the Meta description tag, you can write an accurate description of your website. Preferably include your main keyword phrase in this description. This is what will appear in the search engine results pages. Otherwise Google will grab a random snippet of text off your website to use as a description, which may not be ideal.

The Meta keywords tag will probably not prove very useful. As mentioned above, the search engines no longer place any importance on these keyword phrases. Can it hurt to include them? Probably not, unless you aggressively stuff your keywords into them. If that happens, your site may be penalized and fall in the rankings.

Here is the code you will need to include in your HTML file. If you use a WYSIWYG editor, pull up the HTML or "source" tab and you should be able to easily edit it. (don't be intimidated —it's really not as complicated as it seems!)

```
<head>
<title>Discount Jewelry Store —Discount
Turquoise Jewelry, Discount Gold
Jewelry</title>
```

<meta name="description" content="Get the best deals on the net at our discount jewelry store">
<meta name="keywords" content="discount jewelry store, discount turquoise jewelry, discount gold jewelry">
</head>

Sitemaps

Sitemaps are used to notify the search engines of each page on your website. Depending on your linking structure, Google may or may not be able to find its way to each individual page. A sitemap is sort of like a "table of contents", a list of hierarchical links to each page on your website.

It's a good idea to have a sitemap as it will allow for quicker crawling and indexing from the search engines. It can also prove beneficial to your visitors in some cases, as they can browse the list to look for a specific page.

If you have a static HTML website, you'll likely have to create your sitemap yourself, coding it by hand or in your HTML editor. It may take some time and effort, but it'll be worth it in the end.

A good way to lay out your sitemap is by making a simple hierarchical list using the UL and LI tags (bullet lists). Each item on the list should be a link to a page on your website, and the hierarchy can be arranged like this:

Jewelry

- Necklaces

    - Pearl Necklaces
    - Silver Necklaces
    - Gold Necklaces

If you have more than 100 pages on your website, it's recommended that you create multiple sitemaps.
Once you're finished, save it as an .html file and upload it to your server. Include a link to the sitemap from your main page. You can also upload a sitemap in XML format if you wish. Google Webmaster Tools can help you out with that.

If you have a Wordpress blog instead of a static HTML site, there is a plugin called Google XML Sitemap that will automatically create a sitemap for you.

Blog Optimization

If you happen to be using Wordpress as your blog platform of choice, there are a number of steps you can take to optimize your blog. Wordpress is incredibly search engine friendly due to the way it structures its content. Whereas regular HTML pages are static, Wordpress is considered dynamic.

In fact, Wordpress is more or less specifically designed FOR the search engines, so just the simple fact that you use it to begin with guarantees your site will be quite optimized (more so than a regular HTML page). However, if you don't utilize the steps outlined below, you'll definitely be missing out.

Permalinks

The first and most important setting you need to pay attention to is permalinks. The default setting on Wordpress is to give your blog URLs like this:
http://www.myblog.com/?p=265

There's nothing terribly wrong with an URL like that, but if you change the settings to display the title of the post in the URL, you'll be able to include whatever keyword you're trying to optimize for, which will benefit your blog post's on-site SEO.

To do this, go to the Permalinks tab under Settings and select which kind of URL structure you would like to use.

"Day and name" and "Month and name" are good options and certainly better than the default option, but I prefer to select "Custom structure" and include only the post name in the URL. It's clean and simple. The URL will thus look like this:
http://www.myblog.com/post-name/

To do this, you'll have to enter %postname% as the attribute under Custom Structure.

Titles

The default setting for Wordpress is to create titles like this:

My Blog >> Archive >> My Blog Title

A better option is to reverse the structure so it looks more like this:

My Blog Title >> My Blog

This is important because the search engines place more emphasis on the first few words in the title. Therefore you want to include your keyword at the very beginning of your title if possible, and to do that, you'll need to change the default title structure.

This will require editing the header PHP file. It's not as scary as you think!

Go to Appearance >> Editor and select header.php. Find the code in between the <title></title> tags, and change it to this:

<title><?php wp_title(); ?></title>

Or this (if you want to include the blog name in the title):

<title><?php wp_title(); ?> -<?php bloginfo('name'); ?></title>

If you're too afraid to get your hands dirty and edit the code, there is a plugin called Headspace that will allow you to do the same thing.

Pinglist

One of the unique features of Wordpress is that it will automatically "ping" any services you ask it to every time you publish a new post. Pinging basically means sending a notice to various aggregators and ping servers throughout the internet, letting them know that you have published a new blog post or otherwise updated your site in some fashion.

Pinging allows for much quicker indexing by the search engines, and in some cases may even build a few backlinks to your blog effortlessly.

Under the Settings >> Writing tab in your Wordpress dashboard, scroll down to the bottom and you can add a list of ping services you would like to automatically update each time you publish a post.

To find a list of ping services, conduct a simple Google search and you should be able to find a whole boatload of them. Simply copy & paste them into the text box shown above, save changes, and you never have to think about it again!

Wordpress Plugins

As if Wordpress wasn't awesome enough to begin with, it also offers its users a wide variety of plugins that allow them to customize their blog to their exact specifications. There's a plugin for just about everything! In this chapter, I'm listing the best plugins to install on your blog for SEO purposes.

You don't necessarily have to install all of them. In fact, the more plugins you have installed, the slower your blog will load, which will affect the rate at which search engines crawl your pages. So don't go crazy with the plugins —only use the ones you really need.

SEO All In One

Perhaps one of the most popular plugins for Wordpress, the SEO-All-In-One plugin has many features:

- Automatically creates meta tags.
- Automatically optimizes titles for the search engines.
- Allows you to edit individual post titles and keywords as you see fit.
- Allows you to create a post excerpt to be used as the description in search engine listings.
- Contains a no index option to prevent the search engines from indexing possible duplicate content on the archive, tag, and category pages.

Google XML Sitemap

Another popular plugin, the Google XML Sitemap plugin automatically creates a sitemap for you. This takes A LOT of work out of your hands, as creating a sitemap can be a long and arduous process, especially if you have lots of pages on your site. A sitemap will ensure that the search engines have access to each individual page on your website, leading to faster and more complete crawling and indexing.

Related Posts

The Related Posts plugin lets you put a list of Related Posts at the bottom of each blog post. This improves the navigation of your blog and keeps visitors sticking around for longer.

It gauges relation primarily through tags. If you've written a blog post about Improving Blog SEO, some of the Related Posts might be:

- Best Wordpress Plugin for SEO
- How To Customize Your Blog for Improved On-Site SEO
- On-Site Blog Optimization Tips

Robots Meta

The Robots Meta plugin will create a robots.txt file for your blog in addition to modifying meta tags when necessary. Robots.txt tells the search engines not to index specific pages.

The number one reason you'd want to block certain pages from being indexed is because of duplicate content. Wordpress Archives, Tags, and Categories pages all contain content that exists elsewhere on your site. By telling Google and other search engines not to index these pages, you can avoid facing a duplicate content penalty.

This Robots Meta Plugin will do this for you automatically based on your specifications.

WP-Cache

The WP-Cache plugin has one purpose: to speed up your blog! If your blog is slow and lumber some, the search engine spiders will have a hard time crawling it. Plus your visitors might get frustrated and leave.

The WP-Cache plugin works by caching all of your Wordpress pages in one single file. When a request is made, the pages are accessed through this file rather than by loading and compiling each of the PHP elements from the database.

Off-Site Optimization

Okay, so you've learned how to properly optimize your website. However, on-site optimization may not be enough to gain significant rankings, particularly if you're up against some stiff competition. To really compete in the "Wild West" of the internet, you're gonna need some high quality backlinks. Lots of them!

Backlinks are simply inbound links leading to your website from other sites. If you have a lot of backlinks from external high PR websites, Google will deem your website popular and important. Think of backlinks as building your reputation.

With zero backlinks, the search engines don't know what to think about you. You're not important, and for all Google knows, you could be a spammer! But some nice backlinks from sites that Google already favors will change this perception around. If a powerful, high-authority website is linking to yours, it must mean that there's something special about your website.

The more backlinks you have, the more weight Google will give your website in the search results. Always try to include the keyword you want to rank for as the anchor text.

Don't build backlinks too quickly or you may be penalized. Make a habit out of steadily building 5-10 backlinks a day.

Here are some fairly easy ways to gain backlinks:

Forum Signatures

Posting on forums with a link back to your website in the signature is a good way to build a steady stream of backlinks to your site. Each thread that you post in will provide a fresh backlink. The forums you post to should ideally be do-follow, meaning that the Google bots will be able to follow the links to your website and count them as backlinks.

Posting on forums related to your website's niche is best.

Just remember: Please do not spam any forums with links, as you will likely get banned. Always post relevant, valuable content to the forums. Doing this will not only ensure that you don't get banned, but will prove to other forum-goers that you know what you're talking about, so they'll be more inclined to click on your link.

Blog Commenting

Another way to gain valuable backlinks is to comment on relevant blogs in your niche. Generally blog comments allow you to include an URL. Whatever you put in the "Name" box will be the anchor text. In some cases you may be able to get away with using a keyword as the anchor text, but most likely it will be considered spamming and your comment will be deleted.

Blog commenting is a good way to build backlinks, but unfortunately most blogs are no-follow. Since Google is the only search engine that reads the no-follow attribute, you can still gain some link juice and increase your rankings in the other search engines.

It's also a great way to drive traffic back to your website. Make a habit of posting valuable, interesting comments on high-traffic blogs and you'll soon notice an increase in your own traffic.

Article Marketing

Article marketing is yet another great way to build backlinks while simultaneously driving lots of traffic to your site. It takes a bit of effort, but most internet marketers will tell you it's worth it. Submit lots of high quality articles with links pointing back to your website and you'll gradually see your search engine rankings improve along with increased overall traffic to your website.

Here's a list of the most popular article directories and their Page Ranks.

Ezinearticles –6

GoArticles –6

ArticlesBase –6 (no-follow)

Isnare –5

Buzzle –5

ArticleCity –5

ArticleClick -5

Overview

By now you should have a good understanding of the importance of search engine optimization and how to properly utilize strategies to gain high rankings and direct as much traffic as possible to your site!

By using the information you find in this guide, you can greatly improve your site's overall visibility and web presence. You won't see results overnight, but with hard work and determination, eventually you'll experience the rush of spotting your website in the top ten results of a popular (and hopefully profitable) keyword phrase.

The best part of all is that you don't have to spend a dime!

Allow me to offer you one final tip: As internet marketers, we tend to get carried away with making our websites and blogs as search engine friendly as possible. We stuff them full of keywords and write for the bots instead of actual human beings.

Ultimately, your rank in the search engines will be determined by the amount of unique quality content on your website. Publishing lots of valuable information and entertainment will ensure your site's popularity with both real human visitors and the search engine bots.